Guitar Rhymes for Little Rockers

Wrriten by — Dr. Hoot

Published in 2025 by Skooler Books

Guitar Rhymes for Little Rockers

Skooler Books

ISBN:9789334262438

Strumming O

1 2 3 4

C F C
The itsy bitsy spider climbed up the waterspout.

C G C
Down came the rain and washed the spider out.

C F C
Out came the sun and dried up all the rain,

C G C
And the itsy bitsy spider climbed up the spout again.

More Book's in the Series

Dedicated to

MY SISTER

Row, Row, Row Your Boat

Strumming **O**

1 2 3 4

C
Row, row, row your boat,

G
Gently down the stream.

C F
Merrily, merrily, merrily, merrily,

G C
Life is but a dream.

Jack and Jill

Strumming

1 2 3 4

C
Jack and Jill went up the hill
F C
To fetch a pail of water.
C
Jack fell down and broke his crown,
F G C
And Jill came tumbling after.

Mary Had a Little Lamb

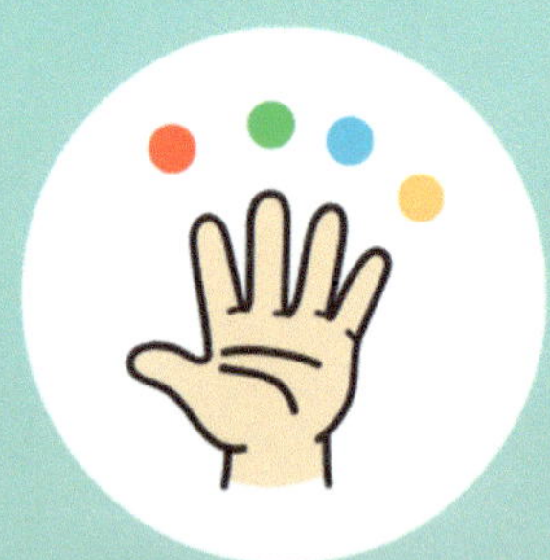

Strumming O

1 2 3 4

C G
Mary had a little lamb,

C G
Little lamb, little lamb.

C F
Mary had a little lamb,

C G C
Its fleece was white as snow.

London Bridge Is Falling Down

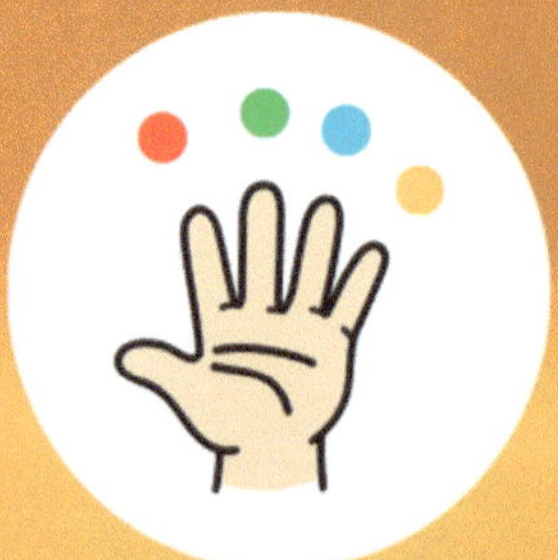

Strumming O

1 2 3 4

C G
London Bridge is falling down,

C G
Falling down, falling down.

C F
London Bridge is falling down,

C G
My fair lady.

Humpty Dumpty

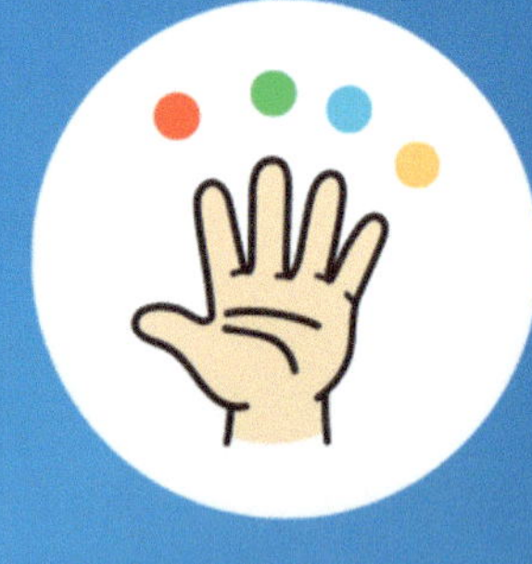

Strumming O

1 2 3 4

C
Humpty Dumpty sat on a wall,

G C
Humpty Dumpty had a great fall.

C
All the king's horses and all the king's men

F G C
Couldn't put Humpty together again.

Baa Baa Black Sheep

Strumming O

1 2 3 4

C G D
Baa baa black sheep, have you any wool?

C G D
Yes sir, yes sir, three bags full.

C G
One for the master, one for the dame,

C G
And one for the little boy who lives

down the lane.

Ring a Ring o' Roses

Strumming O

1 2 3 4

C G
Ring a ring o' roses,

C F
A pocket full of posies,

C G
A-tishoo! A-tishoo!

C G
We all fall down!

Hickory Dickory Dock

Strumming O

1 2 3 4

C
Hickory dickory dock,
G C
The mouse ran up the clock.
C
The clock struck one,
F
The mouse ran down.
G C
Hickory dickory dock.

Rain, Rain, Go Away

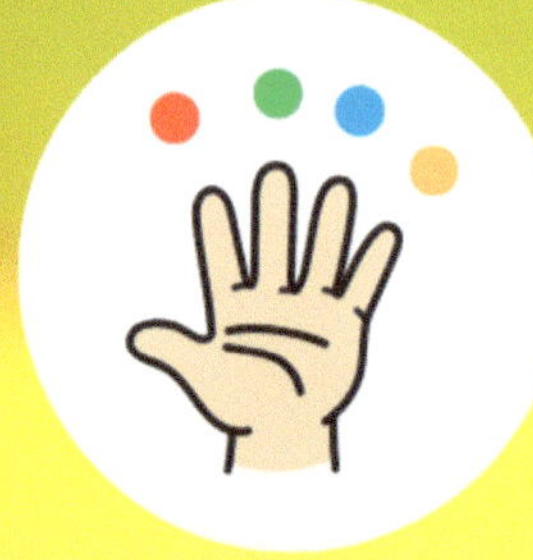

Strumming **O**

1 2 3 4

G C D
Rain, rain, go away,

G C D
Come again another day.

G C D
Little (Name) wants to play,

G C D
Rain, rain, go away.

Happy Birthday

Strumming O

1 2 3 4

G D
Happy birthday to you,

D G
Happy birthday to you,

G C
Happy birthday dear [Name],

G D G
Happy birthday to you!

The Itsy Bitsy Spider

www.ingramcontent.com/pod-product-compliance
Ingram Content Group UK Ltd.
Pitfield, Milton Keynes, MK11 3LW, UK
UKHW061433190726
13845UKWH00021B/171
* 9 7 8 9 3 3 4 2 6 2 4 3 8 *